TEACHINGS

DAVID FISHER

Illustrations designed by

SUSAN FISHER

Frontispiece by K. Rudin

Published by Ross/Backroads Books

Back Roads Books
Box 543
Cotati, Calif.
94928

Ross Books
P.O. Box 4340
Berkeley, Calif.
94707

ACKNOWLEDGEMENTS: Some of these poems first appeared, sometimes in different versions, in the following journals: *kayak* ("The Murderers"); The Carlton Miscellany ("The House"); *Center* ("Come In," she said. "Don't Smoke."); *Back Roads* ("First Amusement," "The Cryptoscope," "Why Do You Want to Suffer Less?"); *Gallimaufry* ("Waldo," "The Violin"); *The Paris Review* ("The Teacher"); *Choice* ("Yellow Sky, Blue Earth"); *Poetry Northwest* ("Contributor's Notes"); Poetry Flash ("A Language of Stone").

Library of Congress Cataloguing in Publication Data:

Library of Congress
Catalog Card Number: 77-71441

Fisher, David
Teachings

ISBN: 0-918510-01-5 Pbk.
ISBN: 0-918510-02-3 Hbk.
ISBN: 0-918510-03-1 Signed Hbk.

Back cover photo by Andrew Gulliford.

for Abraham Lincoln Gehman
for Grace Hall Brown

for Ben Coleman and Sara Gehman Fisher

THE MURDERERS

We sweat in our Sunday clothes, grow sticky
under the trees, before the bell
in the louvred tower calls us in.
The church is full of worshippers and flies.

An old dog pants in the aisle.
The preacher's sermon is long, and in three parts.

I sit in my pew and rage: I tear my brother's hair,
my eyes are open during prayer, I make airplanes
with the pages of my red-letter bible,
I take coins from the passing plate,
I fire imagined guns, throw darts, and javelins,
swing in my mind from the chandeliers.

The bulletins and funeral home fans
beat like sails against the heavy air.
The feeble-minded boy
is catching flies with his hands. Upstairs,
from the loft, comes the low laughter
of the courting couples. The preacher is sure
there are souls who have not come
to Christ, out come the hymnals,
old voices reach for the high notes,
young boys croak the harmony.
Mrs. Laetitia Pulley sings the solo.
The preacher sits beside her, sweating tallow.

I must stop this, I will learn bad words
and scream them, I will stand up and strike
the bald man on the head.

It is nearly finished. Soon I can go home
and listen to the Packers. Threads
of cellulose float in my eyes.
There is a rattle of glasses
and the slight crunch of crackers.

THE HOUSE

It is late, the child is still awake,
he thinks of turnips warm from the fields
and the hog-nosed snake in the mailbox
and the house whispers, "Are you awake,
do you — —?" and he is awake, the day
was sweet and long, there was the yellow bus

with the flapping stop-signs,
the smell of paste,
the construction-paper chains, the steps
of the gym where the big boys smoked,
and the house whispers,
"You are too little, you are like

the dog with his head in the smokehouse,
none of this is yours." And the child
turns his pillow to the cool side,
and thinks about the afternoon,
the dogs asleep in the hard dirt yard,
the shoe by the apple tree with the

black-widow spider in it, the hollyhock
coins in bloom, and the evening had
come slowly, in warm and cold currents,
like diving deep in the lake. ·
"Not yours, never yours," whispers the house.
His father was not breathing right,

and sometimes his mother pressed her hand
to her side. After supper he had helped
to turn the crank for the bread,
his mother rubbed the butter in
with a little brush, and then his father
was snoring in front of the ball game

while his mother read from the
catalogue, tomorrow
he would ask his father. "Tomorrow,"
whispers the house. "Tomorrow
you will still be too little,
and after that you will be gone

and you will not have time to understand,
and nothing will ever belong to you."
The boy thinks of his grandfather,
frail and bearded in a nightgown
provided by the legislature, his false teeth
lost in the darkness of a Mason jar,

sleeping upright because he is afraid
to die. "I am not so little,
not so little as
the dog who climbs the ladder
and jumps into the blanket,
or the yellow chick

that died in the brooder,
or the fawn whose eyes
the raven took. I am not too little."
the house is silent. An owl
on the rooftree hoots,
dark lines of geese cross the moon.

SNOW

The snow falls slowly. It gathers
in dark tufts, like sable. The snow
is falling softly.

You are wearing a maroon sweater
and a black boa tonight, and I kiss you,
for the first time, by the icebox.

> *(Or am I driving*
> *near the Black Forest, where*
> *the side of the frozen hill is littered*
> *with jackknifed trucks. There are*
> *great stones beside the road.*
> *The blind priest urges me to go*
> *faster. A truck is coming towards us.*
> *I lose control and float through the*
> *curve, drifting slowly across*
> *the center line in front of the*
> *oncoming truck . . .)*

We are driving the icy pike
from Cambridge to New Haven. Lights
blink on in the gabled houses,
the snow comes in soft parabolas,
lifting into the windshield.

A pheasant flies through the
windshield, and lies dead
in your arms, the snow melting
from its wings, the tiny bits of glass
in the quivering body. The snow
pours in through the broken windshield,
and piles our coats like fur.

I cannot see any longer, I take
my glasses off, and give them to you
to towel dry.

Our small red car skids softly
into a drift.

YELLOW SKY, BLUE EARTH

The fields are blue.
We gather before sunrise at the barn.
It is already hot.
The crops are wet: the cotton speckled brown,
the tobacco with dark green drooping leaves
and the pink and blue morning glories that
climb on the corn at night.
We wait for the sun to rise, but instead
the sky turns from dark grey to yellow.

From the barn, the hills are blue.
The sky is yellow to the north.

It is very hot.

My father
stands in the fields looking north and fans himself
with his straw hat.

The wind crawls across Mr. Underwood's tobacco.
The sky flaps like heavy yellow canvas
and the hail begins.
It is white.
It smashes on the tin roof, bounces
under the shed, and melts at our feet.

When it stops, the floor of the field,
beneath the green and yellow stalks,
is dark green and steaming.

A LANGUAGE OF STONE

There is a language
of stone, a language
of snow, a language
of water. Light beats
in the temples on the sea.
A white horse passes.
The water rises, and
asks the time.
Snow cannons bombard the valley.
Every door gives on the sea.
A serpent is shaking with heads.
There is a language
of stone, a language
of snow, a language of water.
The frontier is barbed

       with swallows.

WALDO

Waldo's seat was an uninteresting green, that clashed with the countryside. He was not sure when it had begun being Kansas.

Waldo had attempted to think in a transcendental manner nearly all day. He was at that very moment, for instance, remembering favorite passages from Emerson's essay on The American Scholar. He was also, as an additional duty, considering the vast untapped potential of America himself.

Unfortunately, part of the vast untapped potential of America included the woman beside him, who smelled of sausages, and talked incessently of Ireland, where, it appeared, she had never been.

It was difficult. It was certainly difficult. Yet he had a feeling Emerson himself would have purchased a Greyhound Ameripass, had the opportunity presented itself.

Waldo became aware that he was not feeling well. Something vaguely to do with his chest.

And this, somehow, reminded him of the only real annoyance in his life — which was that he hated his students. This feeling of his, which was quite distinct, and rarely varied, sometimes disturbed him. He was by no means certain Emerson had hated *his* students — in fact, there was some evidence to the contrary.

But how could one help hating students? One was brilliant, one lectured, one distilled the great ideas. One made the most marvelous connections, one was wide-ranging, and subtle. And the students sat dumbly listening, and took their pathetic little notes, and wrote their pathetic little essays on homosexuality in Alcott, and it was more than a thinking man should have to bear.

Kansas was beautiful. There were silos, and the fields

were silver-green. But Waldo was not noticing the landscape. Some peculiar disturbing intensity was coming over him. He went to the tiny restroom in the rear of the coach, and found himself lurching. The intensity began to concentrate in the area of his upper chest.

And Waldo sought to concentrate on Emerson: and nothing of comfort came. All he could remember, suddenly, was the passage about mad Nancy confined across Concord brook. Waldo began to tremble.

There was a sign in the front of the bus, in bright red lighted letters, a strange Faustian legend, WATCH STEP DOWN, and Waldo found himself gripped by the sign. Drowsily Waldo attempted to parse this legend, but his chest was aching, and his usually sharp mind was bewildered. WATCH STEP DOWN. Was DOWN an adverb? An adjective? A predicate nominative? Was STEP the object of the verb? WATCH STEP DOWN. The sign grinned down at him. The sign refused utterly to conform to the laws of grammar, and would not, Waldo was increasingly convinced, have given a damn for Walden Pond or Nathanial Hawthorne's flute. There was something devilish, Faustian, sly, circuitous here, something larger than grammar. And the sign was somehow a warning to him, Waldo. WATCH STEP DOWN WATCH STEP DOWN

The pain in Waldo's chest was increasing, and was joined by a pain in his left elbow.

The woman next to Waldo who smelled of sausages and had never been to Ireland took this opportunity to spill an unknown fruit juice on Waldo, from a DRINK UP AMERICA mug in red, white, and blue. She received this fruit juice for fifteen cents at every Greyhound stop.

Waldo, who was now sweating heavily, made a grim attempt to think his way through "Self-Reliance." But Waldo's chest, that iron string, hurt like the devil, and his hatred of his students suddenly came over him like a wave. What did they know about Emerson, the Alcotts, Isaac and Mary Goose, Fruitlands? What did they care? Rotten spoiled little glib little bastards. Waldo's breastbone began to throb.

There was a tautness in the sky, and lightning flashed in the south. Waldo's left arm became numb. And just then, with total suddenness, and for no reason at all, straight in the midst of his pain, Waldo began receiving sense impressions.

He looked at the color of his seat. Then he looked at the Greyhound driver's grey cap. Next he noticed the girl across the aisle. He began watching suitcases. The bus was traveling behind a red truck. There was a silver silo to the north.

The profusion of details began to be a little frightening. Where did one stop looking? There was a richness about the Kansas landscape with which he was, as yet, uncomfortable.

Some essential spiritual change was coming over Waldo, and he feared it more than the death he expected.

One last time, Waldo attempted to recite from Emerson: "By the rude bridge that arched the flood..." But he found he could not get past the word RUDE, which swam in giant letters, and led relentlessly back to the Faustian sign, WATCH STEP DOWN.

Waldo knew he was having a heart attack. But the world had never been so beautiful. The thin transcendentalism of Waldo's teaching bellied in the Kansas wind.

Waldo had undertaken, at last, the real Emersonian enterprise — to observe the world.

The landscape was infinitely varied. To the west, the bus faced a sun shining low on the horizon. To the north, the sky was warm with heat lightning. To the south, the tight forked lightning, and a storm. All this to Waldo was a matter of wonder. He felt that one might love or at least deeply respect Kansas. On the right of the bus, the windows were merely streaked, while on the left, the rain struck the windows in quite a different way. Waldo noticed the difference eagerly.

Waldo had pain in his chest, in his arm, in his jaw, and it was his own opinion that he was likely to die, — but there was something hard inside him which had uncurled,in this bus, so that he felt almost grateful.

On the Kansas road there were signs in the warm, slanting rain, MERGE, MERGE. Waldo merged. The drops of rain on both sets of windows began to dance, began to jig, and then all the drops of rain were dancing, up, and then down, self-evidently for Waldo's benefit.

Waldo's mind turned to his luggage, which contained a pint of Hans Kornell brandy, intended as a gift for a maiden aunt. Waldo rose, his hand on his heart, and went in search of his luggage; as he made his way painfully down the aisle he thought of the beauty of Kansas.

Waldo found the Kornell brandy, which he had bought because he knew Hans Kornell personally, and concealed it cleverly within a scholarly magazine. Then he lurched toward the rest room.

He emerged without the scholarly magazine, worked his way back toward his seat, and startled the DRINK UP AMERICA lady by tilting the rest of the Kornell brandy up in plain view. His heart was beating regularly, in fact, felt warm and full, and the pain had subsided.

Kansas was every shade of silver and green. In the twilight, every different kind of weather was softly visible. Waldo was relaxed and observant. The bus moved on in a soft rain that Waldo, his mind sublimely empty of Concord, found infinitely comforting. For an extremely long time Waldo watched the left wind-shield wiper go faster than the right. Then for a long time he simply watched the grey cap that hung behind the Greyhound driver.

Finally he began to think about his students.

JEU DE PAUMES

After twenty years
the same small guard
was on duty
at the Jeu de Paumes.

He got up from his rattan chair
to warn my children:

> *"Petits messieurs, vous vous trouvez*
> *dans une* **musee** *ici.* "*

I asked him
where the little Degas was
that used to stand by the stairs.
He was pleased to be asked.

FRIENDS

The balloon leaves the child's hand.
As we drink coffee,
near the hospital,
near the Bourse.

The distance between the child's hand
and the balloon
increases. Toward the Cathedral of
Chartres the balloon makes its way, pauses,
for a moment, to try the 12th century glass,
and continues on its way.
The child gives a small cry.

> *I am thinking of Ella Fitzgerald's lyrics:*
> *"He gonna turn me down and say can we*
> *still be* friends.*"*

And I wonder if the child and balloon
will ever be friends again, if there is *ever*
any affection after the fact.

RAIN, ARBORETUM

Each tree and
bush has its
patter:
Monterey cypress
different from
monkey puzzle
twinflower different
from spicebush
(scent from the
wide open calyx
of the strawberry)
...The Latin
names continue
as each living
thing says welcome.

1er DIVERTISSEMENT
by Jean Cocteau

Il y eut d'abord une corrida bien étrange.
Le taureau avait une tête de jeune homme et de
nombreauses frisures blondes sur le front.
Il etait blanc, s'agenouillait et refussait le jeu.
Personne ne s'apperçevait du prodige sauf l'oiseleur au
premier rang des places d'ombre. "Mais c'est un
jeune homme!" crait l'oiseleur. Des Espagnols
en sombrero et au visage bleu le firent taire. De
ce moment lui et le taureau se regarderent et
pleurent en silence.

FIRST AMUSEMENT
translated from the French
of Jean Cocteau by David Fisher

*There was at the beginning a very strange corrida.
The bull had the head of a young man and numerous
blonde curls on his forehead. He was white, knelt
down, and refused to play. No one noticed this
prodigy — except for a fowler, in the first rung of
the shadow seats. "But that's a young man!" cried
the fowler. The Spaniards, wearing sombreros and
blue faces, made him shut up. From that moment he
and the bull watched each other, and cried in silence.*

LE CRYPTOSCOPE
by Jean Cocteau

J'en tremble encore. Dimanche j'avais voulu
fabriquer un periscope de fortune avec des vielles
boîtes a faux-cols et des miroirs de poche. Il y
avait des trous pour les yeux. Mais, par suite
d'une erreur de construction, que vis-je? La mort!
La mort toute petite et très en relief, allant,
venant comme chez elle.

THE CRYPTOSCOPE
*translated from the French
of Jean Cocteau by David Fisher*

*I'm still trembling from it. Sunday I had
wanted to make a periscope of fortune with old
boxes of false collars, and pocket-mirrors.
There were holes for the eyes. But, by an error
of construction, what did I see? Death! Death,
all little and in relief, coming, going, as
though at home.*

THE TEACHER

When I was a teacher
I taught the students that
the two great levelers are
Pestilence and Disease, and then
a few days later I would ask the students
what the two great levelers are,
and they would answer, "Disease
and Pestilence," and I would lose
my temper, and roar, "No, that
is wrong, it is Pestilence and Disease."
They were hopeless. And I would teach them
the structure of tragedy, and I would
diagram the structure on the blackboard, thus:

They did not understand, some
did not even copy down the diagram.

*

I have retired, now, to my father's
small stump farm. I eat cress, berries, cattail sprouts,
and chives, but mostly mushrooms: orange chanterelles
and Zeller's boletus that I gather in gunny sacks.
I fry them, boil them, broil them, pickle them, and
eat them raw. They make me somewhat dizzy.

*

The hogs crowd round the stove,
a possum hangs from the hall tree.
Under the cabin, goats browse
the dynamite.

A new spring came up in a field
and I took a shovel
and I tried to coax it
nearer the house, but it dived
down a badger hole and disappeared.

*

I have put up chintz curtains. In the
appalling heat, under the socket moon,
I worm the corn. When I was a student,
I went to Wales, to Mynydd Llanybyther, and Cwmpidlfach,
I stayed with Thurlow Craig, who told me
country stories, of the dance of the stoats,
of rooks who breed on the midden, of the fox
who played dead to catch the buzzard.
At night we visited the local, in a cart
drawn by a pedigreed Cardigan cob.

I make my own beer now, with
good English malt, I add the hops
in an old stocking my wife left. Sometimes
the hydrometer tells me it is thirty proof,
sometimes, in the moonlight,
a bottle explodes, rattling the windows.

I wear a miner's helmet to bed
Still I have bad dreams.

*

It is winter
The landscape is set forth
like the best blue china.

A young frost makes her
first sketches on the
panes of my cabin

Someday I should like to teach again.

Outside, on the cold roof of my Nash,
I hear the frosty clatter of goat hooves.

AMENOPHIS

Long ago in the city of Sumer
Amenophis ruled. The priests decreed
that darkness
>   *is purely formal*
but the king rose trembling
during these white nights.
The hieroglyphs tell us little more.

The king was no warrior,
his library was
>   *known in the East.*
When sleep was denied him,
he observed the stars.

The neighboring kingdoms
rose with the flooding
>   *of the Nile.*
Amenophis sent his sons to Crete,
and died. There are few scrolls and artifacts
from the rule of this mild king.

THE WOMAN

translated from the Italian of Umberto Saba

When you
were young you could
sting like a blackberry thorn. Your foot,
too, was a weapon for you,
o my savage.

You were hard to take,

Still

you are young, still
you are beautiful. And the knots
of the years, and those of sorrow, have bound
our souls, and made them one. And no longer
in your most black hair which my fingers gather
must I now fear
your small white faun-like sharp-pointed ear.

"COME IN," SHE SAID. "DON'T SMOKE."

"Come in," she said. "Don't smoke." "Sit
over there." Her will was active, fluttering, welcoming
his opposition. He did not oppose her.

"I don't understand your recent work . . . shall
we go to lunch?" "Where shall we got to lunch?"
He indicated no preference. She proposed a restaurant.

He also had no preference as to whether they should
visit the library before or after lunch, or as to
whether they should take 17th or Clipper to the
restaurant. He kept his eyes down, and had no
preferences; he thought of himself as a stone, to be
shaped by the tumultuous waters of her will.

They came to the restaurant, and parked in a spot
which she thought might be apposite for this time of
day. They went inside . . . and here was a confusion;
for although she had selected the restaurant at which
they were to dine, and the route which they would
take, and the table at which they were to sit, she
had decided (without warning) to allow him to choose
which chair she should sit in — as though there were
limits, after all, to the passivity he was allowed.

He raised his eyes from the floor. He raised his mind
from the rock. He was startled to find his opinion
called for. He seated her, as best he could, and
noted that her bewilderment was genuine.

WHY DO YOU WANT TO SUFFER LESS?
from *Fisher In Grad School*

I go to school.
The intellect is the cigarette
that makes me hungry.
My new duality arranges her skirts
between tricks.

Dragged-in terminologies,
obese fogs ready for frying,
my mind, inflamed, bloats on distinctions,
the world is drowned,
the future becomes
a monotonous instrument.

Decorous poetry.
Good wives peopled
            with swallows—
            bituminous rivers.

My thoughts,
trained to bifurcate like a seal,
are a form of sewage.

            "I thought there were some
            nice plays on sound—'video'
            and 'fidelity.'"

            "I picked up a sense of penetration
            through repression."

I can no longer reply
with one green word.
I am ready for shock.

My mind has lips like a claymore.
My mind is a whore.
My mind has murdered my suffering.

THE VIOLIN

Both had low-paying jobs, and therefore considered themselves to be artists. She was his intellectual superior, having had to dance in the streets at the age of fourteen. But the two of them were too nearly alike to be absolute friends.

They had been scheduled to perform a biological act together, that afternoon. Since the biology was somehow lacking, they went to the Aquarium instead.

Her ploy was to move swiftly past the exhibits and complain of claustrophobia. His ploy was to creep along, copying odd bits of data to stick in his Writing. The two were on the verge of seriously disgusting one another when they emerged past the dolphins back into the park.

Here diplomacy reigned. He knew that the trees were Dutch Elm and sycamore; she contributed the fact that the process of "pollarding" gave the trees their distinctive shape and decorative peruke.

They sat on the grass, beside two adorable miniature dachsunds, and listened to the concert in the shell. There was "Swan Lake" and several pieces more difficult to identify but which each instinctively felt was progressive.

Their one shared perception involved an elderly man with a cane and a weskit who was deriving the most intense pleasure from everything he saw or heard, as though he had come back from death to teach the world to enjoy itself.

But soon she found she also had agoraphobia. She communicated this to her friend — to whom this concert was the peak of a day which he had no reason to suspect of getting any better. He left reluctantly.

That night, sleepwalking, he strangled his favorite violin.

THE BEAR

Thrown from the boxcar of the train, the bear
rolls over and over. He sits up
rubbing his nose. This must be
some mistake,
                              there is no audience here.
He shambles off through the woods.

The forest is veined with trails,
he does not know which to follow.
The wind is rising, maple leaves turn up
their silver undersides in agony, there is a
smell in the air, and the lightning strikes.
He climbs a tree to escape. The rain
pours down, the bear is blue as a gall.

                              *

There is not much to eat
in the forest, only berries,
and some small delicious animals
that live in a mound and bite your nose.

                              *

The bear moves sideways through a broom-straw field.
He sees the hunters from the corner of his eye
and is sure they have come to take him back.
To welcome them, (though there is no calliope)
he does his somersaults, and juggles
a fallen log, and something
                              tears through his shoulder,
he shambles away in the forest and cries.
Do they not know who he is?

*

After a while, he learns to fish, to find
the deep pool and wait for the silver trout.
He learns to keep his paw up for spiderwebs.
There is only one large animal, with trees
on its head, that he cannot scare.

*

At last he is content to be
alone in the forest,
though sometimes he finds a clearing
and solemnly does his tricks,
though no one sees.

DAVID HALL

When the three of us came
down the hill to visit
Uncle David, he would always
be there on the back porch with
the big conch shell and the
rifle in his lap. We would

follow him as he
wheeled through the house to the
front porch, where we would
always visit. There was
beer in the ice box, and the ammunition
was stacked on the porch. Uncle David

owned a real squirrel rifle, the same
rifle that Loosh had used
to stay out of the Civil War.
The trouble was, the farm
had got too big to shoot across. That old
squirrel rifle wouldn't reach across,

down the valley, all the way
to the Tuckaseegee River. So Uncle David
had another rifle, with a
big scope on it, for the
times when we would come. That was
maybe why we were never anywhere

but on the front porch (and, maybe, Uncle David
didn't mind letting the three of us sit and look
down into his half of the valley and think
about any one man owning any such a farm). My father
and Uncle David drank the beer, and Uncle David would
ask my younger brother or me to take

a case of empties down to the river and set
the bottles in, one at the time, for them
to shoot at. You had to lean
the bottle just right, and spin it a little
to get it to float. Whichever one of us
was down there had to wait to let the bottle go

until Uncle David blew the big conch shell.
I am not sure Uncle David
was my real uncle, but I was named
for him. His real name was
David Hall. He was congressman to
Washington from Webster, and he was re-elected,

though he spent, by my father's count
about eight of his childless years in
some kind of hospital. When Uncle David blew
the big conch shell, one of us would lean
a bottle just right, and spin it a little, and
let it go. When we had done it just right it would

slip on across the valley, and they would
shoot down at it. Whoever was shooting
had to get the bottle before it hit the rapids,
because the rapids made it too hard, and because
there had been some complaints from the other
side of the valley about ricochets

off the church steeple. My brother and I took turns
setting up the bottles, and my father and Uncle David
took turns shooting them. Uncle David
hit nearly half of his. My father
almost never hit a single one. Uncle David would
laugh and hit my father on the leg and say

"Hoyt, you just can't shoot." Then my father would
laugh, but I would have to go beat up
my little brother, because — *shit!*
My father could
shoot the eyes
out of a lizard.

I was going to tell Uncle David
that my father could shoot
when I went to see him in the hospital two days
before he died, but I didn't, because by then
he was little as that conch shell, and because
he always used to give me at least a quarter

to set his empty bottles in the river.

OF THE PAUCITY OF MEMORY

Oh I should like
to be rid of love
of tears, of longings —
of the assassin's heat.
But nothing surprises the altar,
nothing unknots the difficult horses.
I see you clearly
in a long gown,
descending the carpeted stairs
on my arm. My eyes, I suppose, are open.
Beyond us the shadow of a great bone
towards which we descend.
We speak to each other,
again we embrace. We have not
yet noticed the ominous clang of objects,
we have not yet been schooled in remembering.

IN OPPOSITION TO REDEVELOPMENT

They say I am dying, and now
they have left me alone...and you, and you...
perhaps you were the last to go...and now it is
my turn, my flesh is wax like a dolphin's,
and I am not always sure when I am dreaming...
Do you remember the Thanksgivings
we used to have for the old men South of Market,
for the old men dying South of Market,
for the old men they could not even
leave to die South of Market? At last
they broke the elevators, and the old men went away.
And now it is my turn...and I am also alone,
like an old man driven North of Market,
for a new hotel, for a new Stadium,
for a new convention center. The sheets are hot,
I am the subject of conferences. You will
come soon I know, I am sick and difficult, still
you will come. I am aware of trembling.
I have dreamed today of you and of roses. In my dream
the wrecking ball swung through the Milner Hotel,

the dust was everywhere, like snow.
The old men have come and gone...
when I die, I fear they will
fold my small gown and build, in my place, a stadium.
Or a convention center. Perhaps I am dreaming again,
my dreams are not always of you, sometimes I
bleed to death, slowly, and you will not come,
though my blood is like roses. Oh I am grown
so sensitive, I believe I could feel
the touch of your hand on the door. My roommate
died last week, at the very end he cried. I wish
you would come soon, I am so light, and so small,
you could come and take me in your arms,

>   *as though*
>   *I were a rose.*

THE CHILDREN WHOM I HAVE INSTRUCTED

When it is summer and I am dead,
 and when it is
sweeter outdoors
 than in an obscure salon,

they will gather, sometime,
 and make a festival!
with some verses of theirs
 which were lost like the sounds

     of a horn.

CONTRIBUTOR'S NOTES

This is no mere biography — on the verge of
becoming incredible I have ceased to apologize
for my actions. Always and forever my destination
is someone's arms. If these small boats help me
get there, then I am glad to have written them
and glad too that you have sailed them towards
me. Language is an extended pronoun, the
existence of which proves nothing but a point
of view. As with myself I love it and I seek
to destroy it.

1.   I have always wanted to meet someone
who was on the verge of becoming incredible.

2.   Your small boats are a definite argument
for mass transit.

3.   Would you mind getting out of my arms?

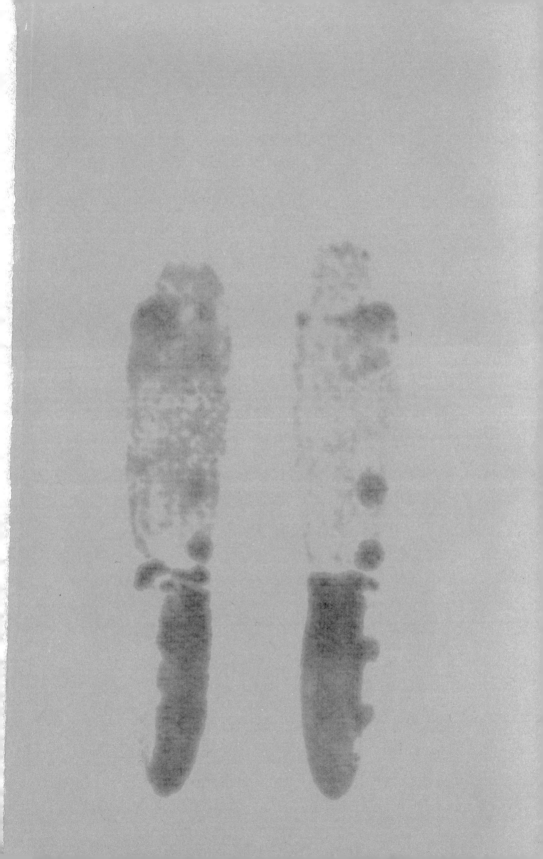

79575   PS
                                   3556
                                   I812
                                   T4

FISHER, DAVID
    TEACHINGS.

DATE DUE